The ENGLISH LANGUAGE

The ENGLISH LANGUAGE
by Alex English

with Gary Delsohn

CONTEMPORARY
BOOKS, INC.
CHICAGO ■ NEW YORK

Denver Nuggets' photos by Debra Curi and Mary Tiernan.

Published by Contemporary Books, Inc.
180 North Michigan Avenue, Chicago, Illinois 60601
Manufactured in the United States of America
Library of Congress Catalog Card Number:
International Standard Book Number: 0-8092-4827-1

Published simultaneously in Canada by Beaverbooks, Ltd.
195 Allstate Parkway, Valleywood Business Park
Markham, Ontario L3R 4T8 Canada

Dedication

To my family and especially to the memory of my grandmother

Contents

A friend said recently that Alex English has become a dominant force in the NBA yet does his work in "a small office," just a few feet wide on the right side of the basket. It's as if everyone in the arena knows the move he wants to make and he still can't be stopped. Alex can do a lot more than just score from the right side of the floor, but he's so meticulously good at that, it's what he's become known for. The man is a poet on and off the court and one of the true "class acts" in all of sports, someone who reflects well not only on the fine game of basketball but also on himself. In this age where we all seem to worship self-indulgence and promotion, Alex represents himself and his sport with a quiet but intense dignity that rubs off on all of us.

Gary Delsohn, co-author

Introduction

I know that most people think of me as a quiet, steady player—someone who can score a lot of points, but not someone who's known for flash and flamboyance. And I must admit, that description bothered me early in my career. It's the more flamboyant players who get the recognition and the big salaries, and I felt I was not getting what was due me for the kind of player I am. But after 10 years in the league, it's not so important anymore. I think I'm more appreciated as a player who can really get the job done and I figure the people who know basketball know I can play the game. I was really honored last year when *The Sporting News* named me to its "All Crunch-Time Team," the five players who can most be counted on to make the clutch play when the game is on the line. That has come to be my job, and my teammates expect me to want the ball and know what to do with it when we need to score. So it was a real thrill to be named to a team that includes Kareem Abdul-Jabbar, Larry Bird, Isiah Thomas, and Adrian Dantley. That's pretty good company to keep, and it meant a lot to me.

I think I'm actually a pretty flashy player, but in a subtle way. I know that may sound contradictory, but what I mean is that someone watching the game may not realize how much damage I've done or what I've accomplished until the game is over and you see a stat sheet or a box score. I play in a style that may look easy to some people, like it doesn't require that much of an effort. They used to say that about Hank Aaron, the great baseball player, and he wound up being the all-time home run champ. I just don't like to waste a lot of energy dunking, for instance, or making a lot of movements on the floor that I feel are unnecessary.

Sure, I think dunking is good sometimes because it can get a player and a team excited and pumped up. But sometimes you're too tired to dunk. Other times, you're so pumped up to begin with you're too excited not to dunk. I'll do it sometimes. But I won't waste a lot of energy trying to dunk over three guys. That's not my game. I didn't learn to play that way. For one thing, when I played at the University of South Carolina, dunking was banned by the college rules, so it was a part of my game that I never really worked on or got to enhance. And some of those guys who know how to play the game that way probably can't play it my way. They probably have to make a very conscious effort not to dunk the ball, to stop and take a jump shot or make a pass. But that's the only way I know how to play. It's the way I learned to play, the way I was brought up.

You may not believe it, but when I was a kid in junior high school I wasn't too coordinated. My sisters and my friends called me "Flick"—that was my nickname. People I know down in Columbia, South Carolina, my hometown, still call me that. But it wasn't for the flick of the wrist when I shot the basketball. It was a derivation of "afflicted." How's that for cruel? I was very awkward as a kid, an ugly duckling in a way. I was growing so fast, I was all arms and legs. My mind couldn't control my body, which was so long and lanky. I was very conscious of trying not to be awkward, of course, because it wasn't any fun being called those names.

So I worked at becoming graceful. I trained a certain way, stretching all the muscles, especially the ones that seemed to be growing overnight. I did a lot of yoga, which I learned from reading one of my grandmother's many books. It taught me how to stretch the muscles. I still do a lot of stretching exercises most players don't do. I work out on weights a little, especially as I get older, to keep the strength up. But I don't do a lot of that. I don't need to look like Arnold Schwarzenegger. I just want to be equipped to do my job. I also did a lot of running, running on my toes for miles and jumping like a ballet dancer to get the grace of movement, the fluid motion that is so much a part of my game.

When I'm really training hard during the summer to get in shape for the next season, I run in the early morning on the country roads outside Columbia. I look weird, but no one is around that early, so it's pretty private. I run in and out, weaving back and forth, running forward and backward—the kinds of movements I'll make in a game. I think those kinds of exercises all stretch out my muscles and help give me the flow and deceptive kind of strength I thrive on. I think that may be why I don't get all the recognition sometimes a lot of other players do, even though, game after game, I do the same things and sometimes more than they do. I'm not trying to be a braggart, because that's not my style, either.

The style of my game has a lot to do with what I'm talking about. I try to be smooth on the floor, almost unobtrusive. I'm not jerky in my movements. A jerky motion is part of a ballplayer's game, it seems to me, only when he's making a very conscious effort to do everything. When I play, I try to be more fluid. I try to do everything within the flow of the movement on the floor, without much stopping and starting, without much of the herky-jerky motion a lot of big scorers use. It's like trying to be a dancer out there. Everything is one motion. I don't draw a lot of attention to myself that way. And, like I said, I've gotten more comfortable with that over the years.

I think if you knew a little more about my background and the way I was reared in Columbia during the 1960s, you'd get a much better sense of why I play the way I play and why I am the way I am—kind of quiet, not one of the more outgoing players in the league, and certainly not a favorite of the news media. I suppose it all started with my grandmother Estelle, my mother's mother. She was without a doubt the greatest influence on my life and a beautiful, beautiful person.

1
The Early Years in Columbia

A poem I wrote about my grandmother Estelle tells part of the story.

Grandma shared
her wisdom with me,
Grandma told me
to look to God for strength,
Grandma gave me a Love
*   whose plateau*
has yet to be reached
again.
Grandma gave me her backbone
on which I survived
*   and grew strong.*
Grandma instilled her determined self
inside of me so that I
continued my struggle
*   and grew stronger.*
Through not physically here,
Grandma's spirit still lives
*   inside of me. . . .*

I grew up in a very poor family. Eleven brothers, sisters, cousins, all living in a cramped three-room house with my grandmother, the only one in the house who had steady work. My father left us at an early age—he died when I was nine—and my mother had moved to New York to try to find work and help support us. Working conditions and opportunities for blacks in the South during the sixties were very, very rough. Many people moved north to find work, and that's what my mother did. She used to send money every now and then, and little

"Alex English's touch is softer than a baby's fanny." —Buddy Martin, *The Denver Post*, **sports columnist**

packages, but my grandmother was the head of the household. I missed my mom, but I had so many people around me who loved me and cared for me that I guess I really didn't miss her that much.

My mother eventually moved back and married my step-father, who was another extremely important person in my life. His name was Paul Nesbitt, and he was a quiet and gentle man who treated us very well. He was very easygoing. He mixed concrete in a cement plant and he worked very hard to provide for us. This was a man who didn't have to take on my mother and her four kids, but he did. He bought us a house in the suburbs and took us out of the ghetto. When he died in April of 1986, I felt a great loss. Other than my grandmother, he was one of the most important and positive influences on me. He taught me how to dish out love and to accept love.

He took us to that house in the suburbs, out of the ghetto, and he made sure we all had enough to eat and enough of the other things we needed. He had a car, so all of a sudden we could go places. Most of the kids we grew up with didn't have any of these types of things, so he made us feel pretty special. He was a provider and he was very important in my life because he taught by example. He had a quiet determination about him that was amazing. He worked hard to make sure we always got what we needed. It wasn't as if we always had everything we wanted, but because of him we got what we needed.

My grandmother stayed in her old house, so when we fin-

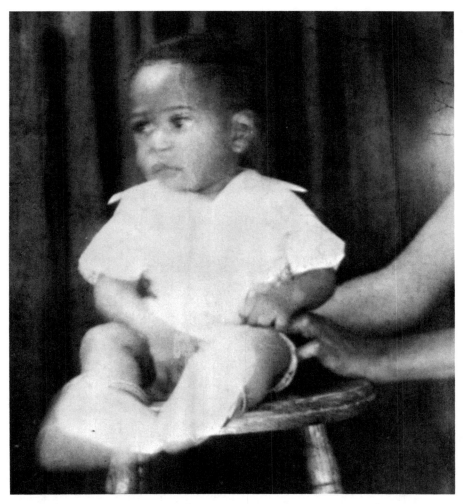

I was always moving, even when I was getting my picture taken at nine months.

ished school we'd go to see her and play over there and wait until my mother picked us up, and then we'd drive out to our own house. My high school coach had to list me living at a phony address when we moved so I wouldn't have to go to another high school.

We were poor, but we had a wonderful childhood. Despite all the rats, the roaches, and the bumps and the bruises, it was a beautiful childhood to me. It gave me the type of determination I have now. I know how poverty is and I don't want to live through it again; I feel as if the poverty gave me the impetus to do something with my life. It's still a very sad thing for me to go

When I was small, my mother Johnnie Mae moved north to find work and help support us in South Carolina.

back to the old neighborhood and see people or little kids who look hungry or sick or are suffering from malnutrition and look raggedy. I don't like to see that. I have lived through it and I try to do something about it when I can.

A lot of kids, I guess, aren't made of the same stuff, and people react in different ways to poverty and everything else they are exposed to. A lot of kids I grew up with went a whole different direction. Some of them are dead. Some of them are

*My sister, Margaret, played basketball
for one of the first professional
women's teams in the country. We used
to play one-on-one when we were kids.*

This is Delores, my other sister.

junkies. Some are alcoholics. Some are doctors. We all went different routes. Some of them have never left the rut they grew up in, and they kind of sleepwalk through Monday to Friday. They live only for the weekend and that's all life is for them. I had a desire and determination to be more than that, and I always wanted to do something good for my grandmother because she was so good to me. All of the kids felt that way about her, and I knew I couldn't be dirt poor if I wanted to do something to make her happy.

LEARNING TO PLAY

I suppose it was my poverty that got me interested in basketball in the first place. We didn't have money to do lots of things, so we played all the sports we could. Whatever season came around, we played the sport. We played baseball when it was baseball season, basketball during basketball season, and football during football season. My favorite sport, actually, was football. I loved to catch the ball and run with it, and my dream was to grow up to be a professional football player, like John Mackey of the Baltimore Colts, one of my favorite teams. I wanted to catch passes and break tackles and drag people into the end zone like he did. About the only major sport we didn't play was hockey. There just wasn't a lot of hockey in the South.

I guess I was about nine or ten years old when I really got serious about playing basketball. We had to make our own court and basket out of whatever materials we could find. We'd scrounge up an old piece of plywood somewhere and nail it to a pole we found. That was the easy part. Then we had to find a rim. An old peach basket usually did the trick. If we were lucky

---

I always envisioned myself becoming a pro football player.

---

we found something like a rim from an old bicycle wheel. It was too big but it was sturdy and worked best. Then we'd dig a hole in our backyard, put the pole in the hole, and play. The yard was on a hill, so it had lots of slopes and bumps. There were a lot of rocks, too. It made dribbling the ball pretty precarious, so we did a lot of passing. But we didn't mind. All the guys in the neighborhood would come and we would play after school just about every day. It got pretty rough sometimes and there'd be lots of fights and arguments. Guys on my street would play the guys on the street behind us. Sometimes we had neighborhood rivalries—pretty intense ones, too.

There were five boys in our house. I had two sisters and one brother, and the rest were cousins. My sister Margaret was quite a basketball player, too, and later, when we moved out of the ghetto, she and I played a lot against each other. In college she played for the top black women's team in the country at South Carolina State College. She later played pro for the San Francisco Pioneers, and she was good. Anyway, I was always in the middle of the pack of boys, as far as age was concerned, which was good because I usually had one of the older boys looking out for me. If I got into a fight with somebody, which is pretty common when you're growing up, I could get one of my big cousins or my big brother to help me out. But I really seemed to find myself on the basketball court. I was growing

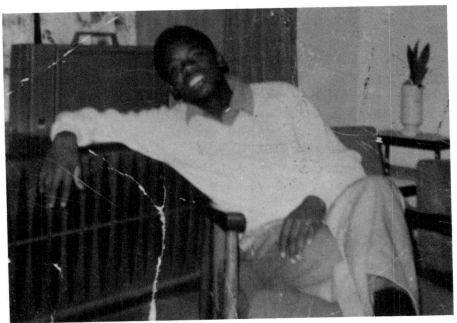

Alphonso, my brother, lives in Columbia and manages an apartment complex I own.

faster than everybody else, so I began to excel. My mother at one time told me I was spending too much time on basketball and that I needed to quit so I could get a part-time job and help support the family. I always did well in school because my grandmother instilled in us a love of learning and reading, but I suppose I spent every spare minute playing ball. School, in fact, was the only thing that really kept me from basketball. But my mom must have thought I was a slouch or something, playing all the time. I just loved it and kept at it.

As I said, I always envisioned myself becoming a pro football player. I really did. When I got to junior high school, I got a chance to participate in both sports in an organized program. The coach, when he saw I had some basketball potential, convinced me to give up football altogether and concentrate on hoops. That was okay with me because I wasn't that muscular and I wasn't into the toughness of football that much. I just didn't like going against all those big defensive linemen all the time.

So I played basketball every minute I could. We didn't have a television, because we couldn't afford one, so basketball was my entertainment. When I was in sixth grade, Sammy Adams, who is my best friend to this day, began playing with me. We started getting obsessed by the sport. We got to the school playground early and played before class. We played at lunchtime. We played after school. On weekends, we went to the local gymnasium. He and I were the type of guys who were never afraid to get into games with older guys because we were looking to excel and could play with them. We didn't know that was kind of taboo and that we weren't supposed to do that because we were younger. But we always got picked and we had some great games. Sammy and I played on the same school teams from sixth grade until we went to different colleges. He went to The Citadel and Newberry College and did well.

I worked hard to improve all aspects of my game. Whenever I went somewhere, to the store for my mother or on an errand, I ran and jumped over all the hedges like a hurdler, improving my jumping and speed. If I was in a room with a high ceiling, I would jump over and over again to try to touch it, and as the years went by there didn't seem to be a ceiling in Columbia I couldn't reach. I always had this fierce determination and drive that told me I could do it, that I could get better and better. So much of that came from my grandmother. It's the same kind of drive and determination I use when I play today, the characteristics that helped get me named to *The Sporting News*'s special team and gave me the strength to accomplish the things I have accomplished.

I went to an all-black elementary school that was made up mostly of middle-class kids. There were kids in my class whose parents were doctors and lawyers and teachers, and they all came to school dressed very nicely, certainly better than me. They all had lunch money. When it came time to pay our fees, $5 a year (I think that was all they were), they all paid them in one lump sum with no problem or embarrassment. But I had to work in the cafeteria to buy my lunch and I had to save every bit of change I came across during the year to pay my fees. I couldn't go to the end-of-the-year picnics that cost one dollar unless I got handouts. I didn't want it to be that way. But those kinds of embarrassments made me realize I didn't want to live like that the rest of my life, and I knew that hard work was my ticket out. I always wanted to do something to make my grandmother feel good and proud because, even with the poverty and the handouts, I was so loved. I had a lot to be thankful for.

I was growing so fast in high school that my mind couldn't control my gangly body.

A TRIBUTE
published in the pages of
THE STATE
COLUMBIA, S. C.
AUG 4 1967

Memorial Obituary

Entered Into Eternal Rest
Friday, July 28, 1967

J. H. English

Funeral services for James Harrison English of 531 Atlas Road, who died in New York last Friday, will be at 4 p. m. Friday at Leevy's Chapel.

He was born in Sumter County, son of the late Irvin Harrison English and Daisy English.

Surviving are his widow, Mrs. Johnnie Mae English; two daughters, Margaret Mae and Delores English, a son, Alexander English; a stepson, Alfonso Glasco; his mother and two brothers, John Thomas and Joseph LesterEnglish.

This is my dad. He died when I was a little boy and I really didn't know him much.

MY GREATEST INFLUENCE

My grandmother was an incredibly strong and decent woman. She taught us about God at an early age. She seemed serene and content and filled with love despite all the problems we had. I have this wonderful image of her that I still get comfort from today. She used to have an old Singer sewing machine, the kind you had to push to run, and I remember coming in and she would be working so hard—she made a lot of our clothes—working and singing gospel hymns. She was so content and peaceful, sometimes I would just sit next to her and watch her, just to be close to her. It made me feel content and serene, too. A lot of times in the summer we'd go out on the porch during the evening and play all kinds of games, like hopscotch and hide-and-seek, until the sun went down. And then my grandmother would gather us all together and tell us stories. She'd tell us about different people in our family history, things that happened when she was a little girl. My great grandmother was part Indian, and my grandmother must have really loved her and my great grandfather because she talked about them all the time. And she had lots of religious and mystical stories to tell us. They were amazing. Everything that happened had a purpose and a meaning. She would also tell us all about the dreams she had and what they meant. I guess she had a mystical side and it was fascinating to listen to her. Some of the stories would be pretty frightening to a young kid, though, and I remember hating to have to be the first one to go all alone into that empty house when it was time to go to sleep. I'd resist and resist until I finally had to go and I'd just crawl under the covers and hide. It's those types of memories that made my childhood special, even though we were so poor. I wouldn't have changed it for the world, because it also helped shape my character and the way I look at things and treat people today.

My grandmother was a very sensitive, generous person, and I know I inherited a lot of that from her. She helped anybody around us who needed help. Even with all the mouths in her house that she had to feed, if someone in the neighborhood was hungry, she'd bring them to have dinner with us. That just meant there was less for us and we were always taught to feel it was a privilege to help others, to sacrifice. And she didn't do this with a lot of stuffy preaching. That approach usually doesn't work on kids. She taught us through her example, by the way she lived her life. She was a presser in a laundry about

Even though we were very poor, there was so much love and support around me that I cherish what really was a beautiful childhood.

three miles from our house, so she got up early every morning and walked all the way to work in the stifling heat, even with her bad arthritis. Boy, she was tough, and she never complained; it was what she had to do to care for her family. The place she worked was only about three blocks from our elementary school and we kids would go by every day and look in the window and see her working so hard pressing her clothes so she could feed us and take care of us. Every now and then she got to come out and give us a nickel or a dime and tell us to get some candy or something. She was always cheerful and happy, even though she was working so hard. She was just a beautiful woman.

My grandmother only had a seventh-grade education, so by some people's standards she may not have been considered very smart. But when she was growing up in the South, it wasn't very important to get an education when you could only go out and work in the fields or get a menial job pressing other people's clothes. But she loved to read and taught us to love to read and learn, too. She used to read us the Bible all the time. We actually had regular Bible classes that she would conduct and teach. She also read to us from a book of yoga with an old ragged cover. I still practice some of the stretching and relaxation techniques I learned from my grandmother's book.

I read anything I could get my hands on that I thought would be good.

But I can't tell you all the good qualities and habits my grandmother instilled in all of us just by being good and strong and loving. I try to live that way today because of her example—quiet but determined, sensitive and kind without looking

LOOKING AT THE STARS

When I was in the fifth grade, I went to the public library and read every book under the title of Greek Mythology. I was really interested in that. I still love to read, science fiction and fantasy for the most part. It deals with things we don't know about, at least not yet. I don't care for detective or mystery stories that much because they're almost predictable. I like to read about things that are foreign to me. I guess that's why if I had a chance to be anything in the world other than what I am now, I'd be an astronaut. I've always wanted to go where no man has ever gone before. I've always been fascinated by the heavens and the stars. The solar system is just an amazing thing to try to comprehend, and I think going up there and seeing the planet Earth just spinning around, with nothing to hold it up, man, that would surely blow my mind.

for a lot of pats on the back or notoriety because of it. My only regret about my grandmother was that she died before I began to really accomplish something with my basketball. I think it would have made her very proud. I was in junior high when she died, it was on the eve of my birthday, and even though she was by far the most important person in my life, I could not bring myself to go to her funeral. I went to a basketball game instead. I remember it as if it were yesterday. I went to see the Marquette Warriors play the University of South Carolina. I didn't think I could take all the pain and hurt of seeing her for the last time, of seeing all the sadness that my family was feeling. I was hurting too. We all were. But I just couldn't deal with it. I got involved in watching the game, but as soon as it was over my mind snapped back to reality.

I suppose that's what I like best about playing ball. It's a tremendous escape. When I'm out there playing basketball, that's all there is. I'm not worrying about what happened yesterday or what's going to happen tomorrow. I'm not thinking about the problems of the world. It's not as pure a feeling as when you're a kid and you're playing. As a kid, you're not thinking about getting hurt or making the team. But it's still fun after all these years. That Marquette-South Carolina game was only a temporary respite, however, and I knew more than ever when it was over and I had to go back home and feel all that pain and suffering, that I had to live up to my grandmother's example. I knew I had to work extra hard to make something of my life. I couldn't let down my grandmother.

2
Getting Serious

I didn't pay much attention to professional sports when I was real small because we didn't have a television and I just didn't get much exposure to them. But when I got older and my mother remarried and my stepfather bought us a house, I would watch whatever basketball and football games were on. Those were the days when the Celtics had their dynasty with Bill Russel and Red Auerbach, and it seemed like the only games ever on TV were the Celtics against the Philadelphia 76ers and Wilt Chamberlain. Bill Russell became my favorite because it seemed like he was always the underdog against Wilt. Chamberlain always towered over Russell and seemed like he could always dominate, but Russell played so hard that he often outplayed him.

Besides Russell, I grew up admiring people like John Havlicek, Satch Sanders, Baily Howell, and Don Nelson, who I got to play for later when I was with the Milwaukee Bucks and he was their coach. I loved Hal Greer on the 76ers. Those were great games. And in football it seemed like the same thing—two teams were on television all the time, the Dallas Cowboys and the Baltimore Colts. I guess Green Bay was part of that, too. So I got to love people like Johnny Unitas, John Mackey, Bob Hays, Joe Namath when he came up.

But even though I gave up football in junior high school, my basketball game didn't exactly take off. In eighth grade I was on the junior high team but I was the last person on the bench and didn't get to play that much, even though I thought I was better than a lot of the guys who did play. I played maybe two minutes that whole year in the 16 or 18 games we played. We had a good team, so I just resolved to practice and practice until I got better and got a chance to play more. Then it happened: between eighth grade and ninth grade I grew three inches. Even though I had some coordination problems because I was

"He has that inner strength. No situation rattles him."—Mike Giminski, Nets center

growing so fast, I could still do things a lot of the smaller guys couldn't. By the time I got to high school I was starting on the junior varsity team and by tenth grade, Sammy Adams and I were the only sophomores to start for the varsity. In fact, we were the only sophomores ever to start for Dreher High School, which had been a real high school dynasty in Columbia. I think we were something like 70–7 during my four years there. I played forward and center but didn't score all that much. I think I averaged about 22 points throughout high school, but I rebounded a lot better than I do now. My legs were a lot younger and stronger. I used to walk all the time on the balls of my feet to strengthen my calves, and it paid off. But I think my game really began to improve after I left high school. You know, basketball really was a godsend for me, and once I realized I could get a free college education through the game, I worked even harder to improve.

GROWING UP IN THE SOUTH

I need to digress a little bit to talk about another very important influence in shaping my character: growing up in the South during the turbulent 1960s. My grandmother was really involved in the civil rights movement and made sure we knew and appreciated what it was all about. She really was an

I've always been a serious person, even back in high school.

admirer of John Kennedy and Robert Kennedy and Martin Luther King. And that filtered down to us. You know, I never saw my grandmother cry in her whole life except when those three men she admired so much were murdered. So we knew we were living through some pretty monumental times, some heavy history.

Then we had our own personal incidents, our own involvements, that still stand out after all these years. When I was really little, maybe around the fifth or sixth grade, my brother and I had jobs selling newspapers on the street corner. He would be at one end of the traffic median and I would be at the

---

Bill Russell became my favorite because it seemed like he was always the underdog against Wilt Chamberlin.

---

other. One day when it was unbelievably hot, we were dying of thirst, so we walked to a gas station to get a drink of water. Well, in those days blacks weren't allowed to drink from the same water fountains as whites or to use the same bathrooms. They were supposed to go around to the back and use the "Colored Only" bathrooms. But we were young and we didn't know anything about that then. So we went in and drank some water from the "Whites Only" fountain. I remember I was so little I had to stand on my tiptoes to reach the fountain. There wasn't anybody out there at the time, so we weren't bothered. All of a sudden, though, this big, red-faced white man came up to us—I can still see the image today—and while my brother was drinking, the man kicked him in the behind so hard it knocked him over. We cried and cried and cried. I wasn't hit, but I cried all the way home, too. We didn't realize people could be so cruel. I learned later he was kicked because we were drinking at a "Whites Only" fountain.

Later, when I was in elementary school, we used to cut through the university campus because it was a shortcut to home, and one time some white guys who had been drinking stopped at a light as some of my friends and I were walking by. One of them jumped out of the car and hit me as hard as he could in the jaw. I was so stunned, there was nothing I could do about it. I don't remember what everybody else did, but I cried again. The frustrating thing was you couldn't do anything

I grew so fast in high school. I was all arms and legs and, I have to confess, I wasn't that coordinated. You can see that by graduation I was towering over the other members of my family.

about those incidents. You'd wind up getting beat up or sent to jail or worse.

There was an incident a lot of people outside South Carolina probably never heard about or else don't remember. It was called the "Orangeburg Massacre," and it happened where my sister went to school. It was when the South was being integrated. Some blacks tried to get into a bowling alley and two of them were shot to death. That shook us up. And I remember staying overnight at my other grandmother's house in the country and seeing the Ku Klux Klan riding down the streets with their white hoods and robes. It was like there was a parade of them.

What really drove it home for me was the separation. There was a street in our town called Gervais Street that was a dividing line between black and white. It was a wide street, and on one side were the nice homes and the white people, on the other were all the blacks. It was unreal to see this contrast. It was something you were always aware of. You could never overlook it. The white people lived well; you didn't. They always had food and nice things; you didn't. They were always dressed nicely; and you weren't. Unless you were a middle-class black. And there was prejudice there, too. The poor blacks fought the middle-class blacks. The light-skinned ones thought they were better than the dark-skinned ones. I'm very proud that we have outgrown that and overcome it. But growing up in such tense, difficult times gave me a lifelong appreciation of the suffering of others. Instead of getting bitter, I try to help people wherever I can. That's why I get involved with as much charitable work as I can.

During Thanksgiving 1985, my family and I were having dinner at my house, and I saw a television newscast about Ethiopia that showed pictures of people suffering and dying. It really got to me. I had been involved with anti-famine work for years, but this really affected me. I knew a monumental effort of some kind was needed to help these people. I thought the NBA should get involved, so I called the players' association and they came up with the idea that all the players in the 1985 All-Star game contribute their shares to Ethiopia famine relief. I think it was $2,000 for each member of the winning team and $1,500 for the losing side. Then the league matched it and later a lot of players who weren't in the game donated the per diem shares they collected during the break. All in all, I think we raised between $150,000 and $200,000, and it made me feel very proud that my peers cared enough about this problem to get involved the way they did.

I can identify with people who are poor and discriminated against. That's why my family and I went to Grants, New Mexico, last spring to be a part of the "Hands Across America" movement. But I guess all of that turmoil was another reason to concentrate on my basketball, something that gave me great satisfaction and something I was good at.

HIGH SCHOOL AND BEYOND

A lot of different people helped me with my game when I was a kid. It was my junior high football coach who told me that walking on the balls of my feet would strengthen my calves. It was my high school principal who taught me that I should follow through on my shot. He actually taught me the correct way to shoot a jump shot.

I learned my own special version of that jump shot in an odd way. There was a friend of mine whom I played against for the state championship. His name was Clyde Mayes and he went to Greenville High School in South Carolina. In fact, we played together years later on the Milwaukee Bucks. In the state championship game, he single-handedly demolished our team. He scored a whole bunch of points and no one could stop him. When the game was over, I sat there kind of stunned, trying to think what made him so great other than the fact he was so strong. I realized that when he shot his jumper, he always got up as high as he could and released the ball at the very top of his jump, making it impossible to block. So I kind of incorporated that into my game. I didn't perfect what I guess has become my trademark shot, the running one-handed jumper, until I got to the NBA.

As I said, we had a very strong high school team. But there were some awfully rough games. One in particular stands out in my memory. We were playing Keenan High School in a tournament for the right to advance to the state championship finals, and their tactics were simply to beat me up. So they had this big center on me named George Williams. He was their best defensive player and, man, he was tough. He kept pushing me all over the place, fouling me whenever he could—he actually spit on me several times during the game. He tried to intimidate me and take me out of my game. It was unreal. We were winning the game and the people in the stands thought the officiating was so bad that they started a riot. The win was particularly sweet, though, because Keenan had been the only team in the city to beat us that year. And it had been on a fluke call that I was involved in. It was a last-second shot as this guy drove to the basket; I blocked the shot—I told you I could jump better on those young legs—and the referee called me for goaltending. So they won.

CHOOSING THE RIGHT COLLEGE

The success I had in high school helped get me a lot of offers from colleges around the country. I don't remember how many there were, but it was a lot. I finally narrowed my choices to Clemson University, the University of Minnesota, and the University of South Carolina. I had never visited a lot of places before in my life, so I was kind of intrigued with the prospect of playing somewhere outside South Carolina. I tried a couple places, like the Universities of Oklahoma and Minnesota, but I finally said, "That's it," and decided to stay right at home. I visited Minnesota in the spring and there was a bad blizzard, so I knew that wasn't for me.

My decision to go to the University of South Carolina was a pretty controversial one. A lot of people I knew were telling me that the University of South Carolina never gave black players on its team much chance to play. They only had two other blacks in their history and just one of them got to play at all, and even then it wasn't much. I was very much aware of that when I was trying to make a decision. When I got there in 1973, there were only two other blacks on the team, Casey Manning and Clyde Agnew. Agnew transferred when I started and Manning, who was my roommate, was getting ready to graduate. So I was to be the only black on the team for a while. Fortunately, they recruited some other blacks, like Billy Truitt and Nate Davies. I was concerned about that when it came time to start college because a lot of people said I would never get to play at the University. But I felt differently. I wanted to prove them wrong. It was like throwing fuel on the fire when I heard stuff like that. I still react the same way when people say I can't do something. I guess I'm just stubborn that way. I just work

Kareem is without a doubt the greatest big man ever to play the game. I'm not sure people really appreciate how hard it is to perform at his level for all the years that he has.

harder. I wanted to prove them wrong, plus I loved my hometown and thought Frank McGuire, a legend and one of the winningest coaches in college history, would give me the playing time if I proved I deserved it.

That was no easy thing, since we had some great players during my stay at USC. We went to the third round of the NCAA playoffs twice, were ranked in the top 20 all but my senior year, and sold out every home game we played. One year we turned down an NIT bid. It was a great time for me, getting away from the ghetto and being on my own, meeting new people, taking interesting classes—I graduated with a degree in English—being independent and playing basketball with a great team.

I broke South Carolina's all-time scoring record with 1,972 points during my last game with the Fighting Gamecocks.

Several guys went on to good NBA careers. We had Kevin Joyce, Brian Winters, Mike Dunleavy, Nate Davies, Tom Boswell. The school was independent then, so we always played the other top independent teams and a lot of the games were on national television. Teams like Notre Dame, Marquette, Houston. I remember playing Houston when they were a real powerhouse and Otis Birdsong was their shortest player at 6' 5". I think their average height was 6' 10". But we killed them. That may have been the best game of my career, though I can't tell you how many points I scored. I've played in so many games over my career that after another one is over it just fades into the background.

A highlight of my college years that I do recall very vividly was my last game at South Carolina, when my teammates went out of their way to feed me the ball so I could break the university's all-time scoring record, which I did, with 1,972 points. That's not that many points, but it's a record that still stands and I'm proud of it. It was really exciting to play in front of all those people and have my mother, who had moved back with us by this time, come to any game she wanted to. There were a lot of advantages to playing at home.

I also got a sense that basketball would become my career when I was drafted as a sophomore in the seventh round by the Indiana Pacers of the old American Basketball Association.

You all know who that is and, no, we're not holding hands; we're just trying to catch our breath.

That really made me start thinking about a pro career. It was a bit of a shock to me, but a real honor, too.

I waited to graduate and compete for the NBA, of course, and continued to enjoy college. I played a much different type of game back then, though. I was considered a big man, playing a lot around the hoop, with my back to the basket in the low post. We did a lot of lob-ins and tip-ins. By playing with my back to

the basket, I perfected my turn-around jump shot, which is probably my favorite and most reliable weapon today. I've shot it so many times, it's a reflex now. But I didn't do much driving or going to the hoop, so when I did get to the NBA, I had to change my game pretty dramatically. Everybody is a lot bigger in the pros, so I wasn't going to be able to hang around the basket and get all those tip-ins. The game is just much more refined in the NBA. That meant I had to work on other parts of my game, learn to move more and drive. We also played a lot of zone defenses in college, but the zone is outlawed in the NBA, so my man-to-man coverage needed some work.

REMEMBERING SOME OF MY COLLEGE COACHES

I've been lucky all through my college and professional career to play for some really good and colorful coaches, and it was great playing for a legend like Frank McGuire. I wasn't as into the history of the game as I am now, so I'm not sure at the time that I appreciated the fact I was playing for one of the most successful coaches in the sport, a national legend. But he was great to play for, a very easygoing coach. He spent a lot of time working on the fine points of the game, but his main focus was on the overall strategy. He let his assistants, like Donnie Walsh, who later brought me to Denver, and Ben Jobe, work on the really fine points of the game. Coach McGuire was a great strategist. He loved to figure out which play to run at a particular time. That's what he was best known for. Donnie was more of the defensive specialist in college and he was a real players' coach. He and I were very good friends, and he is just a very warm person, which may have been part of his downfall in Denver when he was fired and replaced by Doug Moe in the middle of the 1980–81 season. I don't know if Donnie had the meanness to be a head coach in the pros. That's certainly not one of Doug's problems. If anything, Doug, who I think is a great coach, can be too abusively vocal sometimes. But Donnie was never able to effectively separate himself from his players, and an effective coach needs to do that. He has to have that little wall up there that says, "Hey, I'm in charge and you're the players," and Donnie was never able to do that. He cared about people, and he showed it. He's just the opposite of Doug. Donnie hollered and screamed once in a while but he was more of a thinker. Doug is more emotional.

3
The NBA: Welcome to the U.S. Marines

I always thought I would make it in the pros, particularly after getting drafted as a sophomore. When I was in the NBA draft in 1976, the Milwaukee Bucks took me in the second round. After my career at South Carolina, I had hopes of being drafted in the first round and was disappointed when I wasn't. But it really worked out for the best, like so many other aspects of my career, because it forced me to work that much harder. I knew I would have an uphill struggle to make it and I suppose I work best when my back is against the wall. A lot of first-round picks come into the game and they're content. They get three-year, no-cut contracts and they don't feel as if they really have to put out that tremendous extra effort. I never had it that way. I got to appreciate how hard I would have to work if I was to make it in the NBA. My first two years I had to struggle just to make the team, with no guarantees at all. I couldn't afford to take anything for granted.

Being a second-round pick taught me a lesson about how hard it would be to make it in the NBA.

I think I was the 23rd pick overall, and I was very excited to be in the league. But the adjustment was harder than I expected. I went from Coach McGuire, who kind of pampered his players, to Frank Costello, who would have made a great drill sergeant in the marines. He was not a personable coach by any stretch of the imagination. I don't know if he knew how to be personable. He was heavy into X's and O's. Learn this, learn that. I think there were more than 1,000 plays we had to learn, and we had tests. Fortunately, there were enough veterans around to help me adjust to his style and his system. I met my first real mentor there, the great forward Bobby Dandridge,

> *"You don't average 29 points in this league, and Alex has averaged 30 several times, without wanting the big shot. He is awfully tough when the game is on the line."*—**Hubie Brown, coach of the New York Knicks**

whom I really grew to admire and respect. He kind of took me under his wing and was a great example to me, just as my grandfather and stepfather had been earlier in my life, by the quiet determination and strength he showed on and off the court.

Even though I almost got cut from the team that first year because the Bucks had a lot of small forwards, and as tough as Costello was, I had a good pre-season, leading the team in points and rebounding. So I felt pretty good. I was particularly happy when I got the starting nod for the opening game. But I didn't do very well—I guess I was nervous, and the coach sat me down after five or six ineffective minutes. I don't think I played another minute over the next dozen games. That was quite a shock, too. Ever since ninth grade I had been a starter, one of the stars of any team I played on. It was hard, because I really hadn't spent much time on the bench. But then again, I was a rookie and I realized there is a price for rookies to pay to learn about the NBA game. So, reluctantly, I was prepared to do that, even if I felt in my heart that I really deserved to be a starter. That's the way that first season went. Costello was

Because I'm known as a scorer, a lot of teams try to defend me by pushing me around a lot. I guess I've learned to live with it.

I first learned this shot, putting the ball up at the very top of my jump with my arms fully extended, after our high school team got trounced by a guy who had a similar style.

47

under a lot of pressure in Milwaukee to produce a winner and he wasn't about to gamble with a green rookie. He got fired a few months later and my rookie year ended pretty much without distinction. I averaged not even eight minutes a game and just 5.2 points. And I knew with the team having three first-round picks in the next draft and already having a lot of small forwards, things were going to be even rougher for me the next year.

I was determined to buck the odds at Milwaukee. That summer of 1977 I worked harder than ever before to get in

---

I was determined to buck the odds at Milwaukee.

---

condition. I was very disappointed with my rookie season, but I had an inner strength and determination that told me I could make it if I was in peak physical condition. As an extra motivator, I was faced with the Bucks' draft: they chose one of the nation's top college forwards, Marques Johnson, Kent Benson (who they would convert from center to forward), and guard Ernie Grunfeld. A lot of people were saying there was no way I could make it on that team after my disappointing first season, so I was more determined than ever to prove the skeptics wrong. I got a little lucky, too, because Don Nelson, one of my idols from the old Celtics, was the Bucks' new coach, and he liked guys who busted their butts on the floor. And he liked me. In fact, Nellie and general manager Wayne Embry may have saved my career that second year. I also think God had a little to do with it, since the deck really seemed stacked against me.

I always feel as if God has guided me in my career because things seem to fall into place when I least expect it. At this particular time, I was on my way to the arena after pre-season ended, a few days before the regular season was to begin, and I knew I was going to get the news that I didn't make the team. As much as I said I was determined to prove the skeptics wrong, I wasn't crazy. I knew with the strong draft that things would be shaky my second year with the Bucks. We were all over at Quinn Buckner's house, the guard who was the team's number-

You always get up for a game against a team like the Celtics. You also seem to get extra attention on defense.

AM I ONLY A SCORER?

Heck no, I do lots more than score. Scoring is what I'm paid to do, and I suppose that's what people notice and dwell on. But I like to be thought of as a complete player who contributes in a lot of different areas. I'm not as good a rebounder as I used to be, but I contribute there. I get the assists. I will admit, however, that scoring is my specialty.

My favorite shot is probably the turn-around jumper. It's natural to me now. Over the years I've tried the running one-handed jumper, going in both directions, left and right. I've used a running hook coming from the right and a running layup going down the right side. But I can go left, too, contrary to what some people may say. Both Houston and Portland tried to force me to go left last year in the playoffs. The defenders leaned on me with their bodies, pushing me left, pushing me left.

A lot of teams do that too, thinking that I am stronger to my right than I am to my left. I recognize that, but I figure if I can get a step on a guy and beat him right, why not? It doesn't matter if everybody thinks they know what you're going to do if you can still do it anyway. They still have to block your shot or take the ball away from you to stop you. And sometimes I'll fool my man by going left. Everyone knows where I'm going most of the time, but that's the way I know how to do it and as long as it works, I'll keep it up. A lot of guys try to anticipate your jump shot, so you just try to throw something different into it each time. You may fake him, you may not stop, you may keep moving around him. You do whatever the situation calls for and really try to improvise to get that shot off somehow.

I approach the game almost like a ballet dancer, with smooth motions that don't waste a lot of energy. Of course, sometimes I can't always do that.

one pick the year before. Brian Winters was with us when we got a call that said I was to report to the arena to see Nellie and Wayne Embry. We knew this was not a good sign. We actually cried because we were all close and it seemed like the end for me. Brian drove me there. It was about eight o'clock at night and it was a long, somber ride to the arena. Brian dropped me off and said he would be across the street having a beer and that I should come get him when it was over. So I went to the office, feeling nervous and terrible, and there were Nellie and Wayne sitting there with these grim expressions on their faces. I had worked so hard during the off-season that I felt awful about the prospect of getting cut without really getting the kind of solid chance during the regular season that I needed to make it. I fully expected to be crushed, but, lo and behold, they told me they had changed their minds. They said that they had intended to cut me but they decided they saw something in me they felt they could use and they were going to keep me. They were going to put Lloyd Walton, a guard from Marquette who was a local drawing card, on the injured reserve list and keep me. I felt I was in the best shape of my career from all the off-season work, so when the season started I was ready. Nellie made me the sixth man, which also was an adjustment, but I didn't mind because I played a lot and we had a pretty good team. My average playing time more than doubled and I scored about 10 points a game and felt that I was instrumental in the team's success. We played the Nuggets in the Western Conference semi-finals and I averaged about 14 points a game in that series.

Even though I had a good second year, the Bucks and my agent were not able to come to terms on a new contract. I never wanted to leave Milwaukee; I had visions of playing there my whole career. I guess all players think that when they get to their first team. But the Bucks evidently felt I was worth a lot less than what my agent and I thought I deserved. The Indiana Pacers, who had Kevin Joyce, a former college teammate, and coach Slick Leonard, who had liked my game, were willing to pay me a lot more. Slick let it be known during the playoffs against Denver that he wanted me to play for him, but he had to wait until the season was over to actively pursue it. So right after the last playoff game my agent started talking to Slick, and he offered me what I thought at that time was a great

Chicago is a team with a lot of talent that can become a powerhouse if they get some support in a few key positions.

contract. The Bucks offered me a contract for about half as much. They couldn't believe what Indiana was willing to pay, but the Pacers were willing to guarantee it. All that extra hard work and the Bucks wanted me to settle for a non-guaranteed contract! Indiana offered me six figures for each of three years with each year guaranteed and Milwaukee was offering five

---

I always had this fierce determination and drive that told me I could do it, that I could get better and better.

---

figures with no guarantee. I wasn't that crazy about the city, but I loved playing in Milwaukee. I had to think about my career, though, so I left. I signed within 24 hours after the last playoff game.

A SHORT WANDER THROUGH INDIANA

Slick Leonard was another colorful coach. Slick was sure different. He could curse you out mercilessly on the bench, but he was sort of personable. He was a philosopher, in a way. He was always making these grand pronouncements on basketball and life and saying that's the way it is. But he appreciated many of the little things you did on the floor or the extra effort you put into preparing for the season and each game. He was also the Pacers' general manager, so he was interested in the mechanics of the team, of putting the right players together to form a full squad, not in just the day-to-day aspects of coaching.

My time with the Pacers was fruitful, even if it was only a year and a half. I started the first season and played a lot of minutes. I averaged 16 points, and I felt my game was progressing. The real reason I think Slick got me was that I had adjusted to being a sixth man and that's what he needed. He knew I would accept it without any qualms, even though I still believed I should be starting. Though I did start during my first season at Indiana, the next year Slick got Mickey Johnson, another scoring forward, and he figured I would have an easier time adjusting to the peculiar role of a sixth man in the NBA than Mickey would. I still got to play a lot, even if it wasn't as much as the starters or as much as I had played my first season.

But then the same thing happened to me that had happened

I played for the Indiana Pacers for a year and a half before being traded to the Denver Nuggets.

at Milwaukee—I was victimized by the numbers. Indiana had several small forwards so they needed a big power forward. Donnie Walsh, my former assistant coach in college, was with Denver now and wanted to trade George McGinnis for me. I liked Denver whenever I had played there in the past, and the fact that Donnie was there made it even better. But again, I didn't want to leave Indiana. For one thing, I don't like to move. My wife was pregnant and I wanted to settle down and establish some roots. I now realize how hard that is for a professional athlete. But I also felt that the Pacers had the makings of a great team, a championship team, if we had stayed together. We had people like Mike Bantom, Billy Knight, myself, Ricky Sobers, Johnny Davis, James Edwards, Dudley Bradley, Clement Johnson. These were young guys who could play. But they broke us up. I don't think one of the guys I played with at Indiana is still with the team. I was disappointed again, though once more it worked out for the best.

I went to Denver, a city I have really grown to love, got to play for another, shall we say, colorful coach in Doug Moe, who really let my game blossom, and I feel that I have accomplished a great deal here. I also discovered the shot that I guess has become my trademark.

MY TRADEMARK SHOT

A lot of guys will shoot when they're off balance or have no alternative but to shoot because they find themselves in a particular position. But I was practicing one day and started for some reason to shoot off-balance or when my body was in an awkward position. As I continue playing, I am always trying to refine or add to my game so I can keep improving. There are so many strong young guys in the league, you have to constantly improve and work hard if you're going to survive. The running one-handed jump shot was a shot I knew that defenders would have a hard time blocking because I would be running them and shooting the ball at the same time. Playing defense, you have to get your body set if you are to have any chance of blocking a shot. This shot made things a little easier for me because the defensive player wouldn't be able to get set if I was moving and he didn't know when I was going to put it up.

That shot did not come to me quickly, let me tell you. It's an awkward shot and I still have to work very hard to keep it. Like any other aspect of the game, it can leave you for a while. It's almost automatic now, but I still work on it. I work on it during the summers when I play pick-up games in Columbia. Guys like Tyrone Corbin and Xavier McDaniel live there, as do a lot of other great players. So the games we have during the summer give me a great workout, and I can experiment with different aspects of my game. I try to do things that I would do in a regular NBA game. I also work a lot on my defense, jumping to try to block shots so I can get my defensive skills in season

I don't rebound as well as I did in high school or college when my legs were younger. But I feel I contribute to the team in a lot of ways other than just scoring points.

This is our promotional shot from 1984-85 when we were known as the "High Plains Dribblers." We led the league in scoring.

form. You know the offense will be there, so you have to work a little harder to get the defensive game together. Plus, those guys I play with down in South Carolina in the summer are all younger and all they do is run and try to kick my butt. So it's a great test for me.

THE NUGGETS

When I came to the Nuggets toward the end of the 1980 season, I immediately got the feeling that there wasn't a lot of closeness or camaraderie on the team. We had Dan Issel, Bobby Wilkerson, Gary Garland, Bo Ellis, George Johnson, Kim Hughs, Glen Gondrezick. I felt I fit in pretty well. I played against Bo Ellis while he was at Marquette and I was at South Carolina, so I knew him fairly well. But I didn't know Dan or David Thompson or Charlie Scott and the team just didn't seem to fit together. There was no animosity or anything; it just

If I'm double-teamed, somebody has to be open somewhere.

seemed as if everyone went his own separate way. There were different groups of guys who were friends, different cliques on the team, and that all seemed to cause more problems.

David was playing great when I got there, but people were always getting on him because they expected so much of him. He was a phenomenal player, the best I ever saw for his size. I also thought he was a very nice person, a really good-hearted guy. But he had so many problems to deal with that he seemed always to be getting in deeper. People on the team and in the media were suspicious because he was often coming to practice late and getting fined. There were many rumors about what might be the reason, and that just seemed to make things worse for David and the rest of the team. I think if he could have straightened himself out he would still be a force in the NBA today. He was amazing.

Somebody else must have felt the same vibes I did because the next year a lot of guys were gone. Charlie Scott, Wilkerson, and Garland were all shipped out. The team changed a lot and started to develop some chemistry. Moe was hired to replace Donnie Walsh. We got T. R. Dunn from Portland for a future draft choice; Kenny Higgs, signed as a free agent; Billy McKinney, picked up in a trade with Utah; and Kiki Vandeweghe. We started to develop some stability and we also started to put some serious points on the board, winning 46 games, up from 37 the year before.

A JEKYLL AND HYDE WHO WINS

I suppose this is as good a time as any to talk about my current coach, the colorful Doug Moe. Doug is really a players' coach, but sometimes you still have to tell him to shut up. I've done that before, but he just keeps talking. What I mean by calling him a players' coach is that he gives you a lot of freedom on and off the floor. We don't have a curfew or anything like that. We're adults, and Doug treats us that way. As long as you show up to play for him each day, it's cool. That's all he really cares about. The only negative part is that he can be very abusive and aggressive with his language, and I guess I'm putting that mildly. To a new guy that can be very tough to take. A young guy just breaking into the league can get very nervous and flustered by it. I've grown accustomed to it, I've heard it so

I like to think I'm pretty smooth and fluid on the floor, but that takes hours and hours of practice.

much. And every now and then if I feel I need to, I can say something to him to get if off my chest. Once you get to know him and know that he really doesn't hold any grudges, you can do that. But a younger guy who doesn't know Doug and may be afraid of getting cut or not getting any playing time may hesitate about getting it off his chest. The older guys don't hold back. We all express our opinions and that's to be expected if he's going to be as abusive as he is. That makes for some pretty lively scenes from time to time.

Doug has been one of the main reasons my game has blossomed and I've been as successful as I have been the last four or five years. He has given me a lot of freedom on the floor to let my creativity come out. I think I can play a structured, slow-down kind of offense. I did that in Milwaukee and also in Indiana, where we played a pressing defense. But I find this running and passing style to be much more fun—I think it's better suited to the skills I have.

Doug has chewed me out plenty of times. He hesitates on no one, except T. R. Dunn. Someone once asked me if that's because he's scared of T. R., since T. R. is one of the strongest athletes you'll ever see. But that doesn't scare Doug. It's a joke on the team that T. R. is Doug's son and that's why Doug spares him. (I don't know if he takes that as a compliment or an insult.) The real reason T. R. gets spared is he doesn't make that many mistakes, he doesn't give Doug a reason to go crazy on him. But Doug has gone off the deep end on just about everybody else who has ever played for this team, including the trainer. That's his nature. You take it in stride, but sometimes it does get to be a bit too much, and that's when you have to give a little of it back to him to let off some steam.

He's a real Dr. Jekyll and Mr. Hyde. Once the game starts, he's a frenzied, foul-mouthed coach. He's so tense and so hyped up, I don't think he really knows what's going on. It's like he's in a totally different world. But once the game is over and he calms down, he's regular, almost like one of the guys. If he tore into a guy during the game, after it's over he's friends again. I really don't think there's a method to his madness, either, because I think he's out of control when he's doing that kind of thing. I think he's just kind of nuts that way. He'll chew you out sometimes over something that happened three or four minutes beforehand, something that's ancient history in the context of a game. On some people I suppose it works as a

This was a lot of fun: a promotional tour of Europe for Puma Shoes with guys like Terry Cummings and Ralph Sampson.

Our promotional tour in Europe involved teaching the finer points of basketball to some very enthusiastic players in Italy.

motivator. But I think it hurts some people, too. Like Coop. Wayne Cooper is a very emotional player. I mean, we're all emotional, but his is a different kind of emotion, and when he's screamed at in front of a bunch of fans, I don't think he responds the way Doug would like him to. I think Doug should try another approach with Wayne. Coop can be a great player for his size. He can score, he can block shots, and he can rebound. When he's really up for a game, he's a great player. But it's having him out there with that type of effort every night that's the thing. That's what you have to do to be a great player in this league.

OVERCOMING A BAD NIGHT

There are a lot of nights when you just don't feel like playing. When you don't have the touch. I don't know what it is. Maybe it's biorhythms or just the rhythm of your body on a given day. You're out there struggling. Nothing seems to go right. You have no shot. But to be great in this league, you have to replace that with a positive approach and just keep working until you snap out of it. It's not easy. It takes discipline. But all the great players are able to do that. Everybody struggles with it; the great players can overcome it.

Still, Doug is a great motivator in that he prepares us well for a game, for what it takes to win. He gets us pretty worked up about playing, especially the tough teams, which we always seem to do well against no matter how we're playing generally. But Doug isn't an X's and O's kind of coach. We don't have a thousand different plays the way we did with Larry Costello at Milwaukee. He just tells us to play and to play hard. He makes us want to play hard. Maybe the fact that he was once a player helps, especially in his relationship with players off the floor and the respect they have for him.

Doug gets criticized sometimes for being particularly hard on rookies, but I'm not sure that's valid. He just doesn't play

them much. He doesn't treat them any differently in what he says to them or in anything else. He treats them the same way he treats the other guys off the floor. But Doug believes, as most coaches do, that a rookie has to sit there and watch and learn from the bench before he can play and contribute; that there's an apprentice period a rookie has to go through that involves spending time on the bench. That happened to me in Milwaukee. I'm still convinced I could have contributed if I had played more, but that seems to be part of a player's indoctrination into the NBA. Unless, of course, you're a Michael Jordan or a Patrick Ewing.

Having said that, I have to add that I think Doug may have been better off using Blair Rasmussen, last year's first-round draft choice, a little more during the early parts of the season. If Blair had played more in the early games, he could have been much more of a help to us down the stretch. We may have gotten a little closer to winning the division championship because of Blair, who really did well when he got a chance to play later in the year. If he had been given more time on the floor, I think the team would have been a lot better off. But I know Doug was impressed with his play when he did get in, and Blair is determined to work hard and improve. I think we all expect a lot from him in the coming season.

Am I late for English class? No, just shooting a poster for Puma.

4
Sweet and Bitter

As I said earlier, the team began to change about the time I arrived near the end of the 1979–80 season. The next year was kind of a transitional one for us, and it was the only season we haven't made the playoffs since I've been with Denver. Even though the team struggled, I had my most productive season in the pros, averaging nearly 24 points a game, which was 10th highest in the league, and playing nearly 40 minutes a game. That's more time than all but three or four players played, and I felt I had given the team its money's worth. I was disappointed that I wasn't picked for the All-Star game that year. I have to admit I expected to make the team and was anxious to show off some of the progress I had made in my game since becoming a full-time starter and playing all that time. But those honors were to come later and the disappointment was nothing compared to what I felt when the season was over and I almost left Denver.

Being the subject of trade talk is something I have had to deal with all my career. My contract was up and, again, the Nuggets didn't seem willing to pay me what I thought I was worth after the kind of year I had. I think the team wanted to save money and tried to sign me for as little as it could get away with. I was a free agent since my contract expired, so I tested the market. That was something I wanted to do and was just about forced to do because Denver didn't feel I would come back with any offers that would be a problem to them. I had been nogotiating with Carl Scheer, the team president, and the Nuggets were talking about a deal that was well under what I was offered by Seattle when I did test the market. I also got an offer sheet from the Cleveland Cavaliers that was one of the best offer sheets anyone got that year, but I turned it down because I didn't want

> *"Alex has great desire and he can shoot the ball in your face. And at the end of the game, he wants the ball."*—Doug Moe

to play in Cleveland. It seemed there was some real serious interest in signing me for what I felt I was worth, but not from the Nuggets. So I talked with Seattle, and the Nuggets couldn't believe Seattle was willing to pay me that kind of money, even with the kind of year I had.

It's always been that way with me. People didn't believe I could do the job. I'm not really sure why that is. At one point I felt that because of my slim build, maybe people didn't think I could take the punishment and survive the long NBA seasons. Well, I can take the punishment. I feel I am deceptively strong and have proved it year after year.

I really thought for a while that I was headed to Seattle because the whole thing seemed to have broken down. In fact, the Supersonics tried to put something in their offer they hoped the Nuggets wouldn't even try to match. I would have enjoyed playing in Seattle, too. It's my wife Vanessa's hometown and a very nice city. They also had a potential championship team at the time. But I really wanted to stay here.

I love Denver. The fans have been great to me. They really support and appreciate me and that means a lot. I get a chance to do a lot of things in the Denver community and I enjoy that.

We do need some more scoring and a big rebounder and shot blocker to give Houston a real race for the division title. But if we keep all our guys healthy, I think we can do it with our hearts and determination.

People seem very receptive to community involvement from the players. It's a very friendly town. Columbia will always be my home—it's where I was born. But I like Denver so much that after I retire from the game I'll probably make Denver and Columbia my homes, going back and forth a lot. I like it that much. We just bought a new home here, so it's a permanent place for us. It's a good town to raise kids, although it is getting a little too big and crowded for my tastes. I live in the country in South Carolina and I really enjoy the slow, uncomplicated pace and lifestyle. But there's a lot of things going on in Denver. A lot of good culture and restaurants, a lot of good jazz, which I really enjoy. I think the Red Rocks amphitheater has to be the

---

I do wish more people would come out and see us. It helps get the Nuggets pumped up, and I think we're a lot of fun to watch.

---

most beautiful place to see a concert in the whole world. About the only negative to playing in Denver is that, for all the support the Nuggets have gotten, this remains a football town, a Broncos town. It was particularly frustrating last year. After the exciting and successful season we had in 1984–85, I thought we'd really draw some big crowds. Overall attendance was up, but to see only 12,000 fans at those early games was hard to swallow. Especially when there were sellouts in Sacramento or Dallas every time we played there. The fans really didn't start coming out in strong numbers until toward the end of the season. But that's the way it always is in Denver. Anyway, even when the crowds are small, the fans understand the game and support us really enthusiastically, so it's not all bad. I do wish more people would come out and see us. It helps get the Nuggets pumped up, and I think we're a lot of fun to watch.

After I signed that contract with the Nuggets in June of 1981, I was faced with a lot of the same skepticism, and it bothered me again. It was a five-year contract, and a lot of the critics said now that I'd signed it, I would slump, not be as productive. They said I would be too satisfied to really put out. But after I signed

I think we played the Rockets tougher in the 1986 playoffs than the Lakers did.

the contract, I won the league scoring title (in 1982–83) and in each of the years of the agreement I made the All-Star team. Each year they said "This is the year, he'll be too content and lazy. He won't produce. He won't play as hard anymore." Well, that's crazy, a totally foreign attitude to me. I love this game. It's a lot of hard work but I love it. I'd hate for people to think that I'm a slouch because I make a certain amount of money. I'd never do that. It's just not my style. I always want to be better, and I think I have gotten better each year. The same thing happened last season when Sidney Shlenker, the new owner, gave me that new four-year deal. Some people said maybe I got too much money. But the only way I can answer that is to tell

---

I'd hate for people to think that I'm a slouch because I make a certain amount of money. I'd never do that. It's just not my style.

---

you to look at the people who play the position I play and who have accomplished the things that I have. I don't want to sound like a braggart, but I think the facts speak for themselves. The people who play the position I play and do the things I do are paid a lot more. There are guys coming off the bench who make more than I did under my last contract. When I signed this latest contract there was an article in one of the papers that questioned why Sidney Shlenker gave me the contract. Well, I don't feel he gave it to me. I *earned* it and have earned everything I have gotten all my career.

I have always worked hard and will continue to work hard until the Lord says it's time to quit. Then I'll quit—not until then. It bugs me that some people feel I don't deserve this. People are jealous, or feel that athletes make too much money, or just have a negative attitude toward all professional athletes. I really don't understand it. But I have resigned myself to not worry about it much. To be honest, it does bother me sometimes, because I don't feel it's right. But I try not to worry about it a lot.

Ralph is a great player who sacrifices a lot of his natural game for the good of the team. That tells me an awful lot about a player.

This was the first year I made the All-Star team and it's a thrill I'll always remember. I also won the league scoring title that year.

This past year, with the scoring title being contested all season long by me, Adrian Dantley of the Jazz, and Dominique Wilkins of the Hawks, is an example of what I'm talking about. It was fun to be in contention all year, but a lot of people, toward the end of the season when any one of us could have won it, wanted me to put the ball up every time I touched it so I could come out on top. But that's not what the whole thing was about to me. I would have loved to win it, don't get me wrong. I won it in the 1982–83 season and it was a thrill. But it would have been lowering my standards to start shooting every time I touched the ball, just to try to win the scoring title. Sometimes you get disappointed that people don't appreciate

The "easy" ones are great when you can get them.

the seriousness with which you approach the game. You try to have integrity, and if you do, things work out.

Anyway, the current contract, which lasts four years, makes me feel very good because I realize the team now has someone in Sidney who appreciates the things I can do and have done. I felt he was rewarding me, or giving me something I have earned and rewarding me at the same time. And it was really an honor to hear all those nice things he said about what I mean to the team and how I have contributed to the community. That kind of appreciation means a great deal to me and it only makes me want to play harder and do more. Maybe after all these years I have gotten the appreciation I've been after. I'm sure glad I'm still playing in Denver because I'm excited about the team's future.

But before I talk about the last couple of years, the great 1984–85 season when we won the division and battled the Lakers to the wire, or the ups and down of the 1985–86 season when the Houston Rockets knocked us out, maybe it's a good time to talk about another one of my favorite subjects—the news media.

COLLECTING MY THOUGHTS

I think one of the reasons national recognition has been a little hard for me to come by at times is that I clearly am not a favorite of the reporters who cover the Nuggets. Consequently, I think I may have the image of being aloof, uncooperative, or even hard to deal with. But that's not fair. Maybe with the press I stand back a little, but not with the public. Sometimes the press makes demands of you that could easily be avoided. After a game, for example, when you've just finished playing, you come right off the floor, you're tired, you're sweating, your legs ache and you may want to get them iced. Win or lose, you're still collecting your thoughts. Well, the first thing that happens is the press storms in and starts asking you all these questions. You can sit there and listen to them or you can answer. Everyone reacts differently, and I prefer to go and collect my thoughts somewhere. I usually go in the training room, where the press aren't allowed. I stay away from them for a while, catch my breath, and then come back and answer questions. When they're asking questions the minute you come off the floor, you might say anything, since you don't have your thoughts together; you can make yourself sound dumb or ignorant or silly. (Or you can accidentally make yourself sound like a genius.)

THE PRESS

I guess I'm not one of the favorites of the press because I'm supposed to be the team superstar, the scorer, and they always want me to say something. But I want to see my teammates get some of that publicity, too. They've got viewpoints—talk to them sometimes. See what they've got to say, because I'm going to say the same thing almost every time.

"We played hard." "We didn't play as hard as we could." The press always wants you to elaborate, but by nature I tend to be very precise with what I say. I don't say all the things they want to hear, things that make the story. So I usually avoid them for a while, sit in the trainer's room, have a Coke or a cup of water and think about the game before I answer any questions.

Let's face it, even though I know the reporters are just doing their jobs, a lot of the questions are kind of dumb. It's the same stuff over and over. Also, if we're having a hard time and not playing that well, the questions are all about very negative aspects of the team. I don't want to hear that. It doesn't do me any good or make my job any easier to deal with that negative kind of thinking. I know reporters have to address the issues they feel need to be addressed, so they ask questions about those points. But sometimes they get carried away. I remember one point early last season when we were struggling. This one newspaper reporter covering us was negative in everything he said and wrote. It was as if we had absolutely nothing going for us. Well, like I said, I didn't want to hear it. I felt he was going to be that way every time I talked to him, and he was. He was one of those guys who it seemed didn't want us to do well. I think I'm very good at feeling people out, and this guy was so negative, talking about my teammates, talking about how poorly they played, that I finally told him I didn't want to talk about all the negative stuff. From that point on, I think he approached me only two or three times the rest of the year. It was like people were giving up on us because we had lost three or four in a row and hadn't gotten off to a good start. Every team goes through dead spots. But he drew all these conclusions and made all these negative statements to the point where I just refused to deal with it. There are some real good reporters. I think Kevin Simpson, I don't even know what paper he writes for, is a real good writer, a sensitive person. So they're not all bad by any means. But a lot of them do try to take advantage of you.

One last word about the press before we change subjects. Another reason I avoid them at times is for self-preservation. If you do deal with them all the time and answer all their questions and give them what they want, they'll bug you all the time. I have other things I need to concentrate on during the season. If you're chummy-chummy with a reporter, that reporter is going to be coming around all the time. Sometimes you feel obligated to answer questions. Sometimes you're so emotionally high after a game that you don't mind. It all depends on how you feel. But the sportswriters, most of them at least, don't care how you feel. They just have to get their story. And they're going to push you and take advantage of you to get it. They don't care if you're exhausted. They rush in and put their microphones in your nose and say why didn't you do this or why didn't you do that? But as I said, sometimes you feel obligated to respond, at least to the fans. They pay for their tickets and some of them want to know why you did something a certain way or what was going through your mind. So I try to cooperate without being taken advantage of.

THE FANS

As far as the public is concerned, I try to be as responsive as I can. I'm recognized off the floor because the team gets a lot of recognition and Denver is a great sports town. Even though I try to get involved with the community if I feel I can help someone, I'm not in the public eye all that much. I'm not partying on the town at every social event there is. I'm home, with my wife and children. I'm not loud or boisterous by nature, so I don't try to to draw all that much attention to myself. But it's kind of hard to be incognito when you're 6'8". People always want to know how the weather is up there. How long is your bed? It's hard sometimes. But I don't mind being

As long as it doesn't get out of hand, signing autographs is a part of the game and lifestyle that I really don't mind.

Vanessa was a flight attendant. I met her on one of my countless road trips.

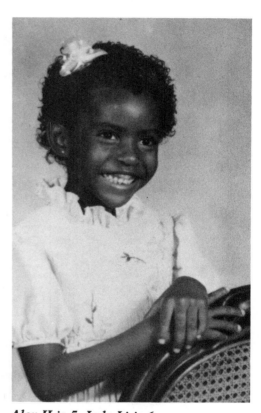

Alex II is 5, Jade Li is 6.

Here's Vanessa with our number three, William.

Being on the road is hard because it takes you away from your family and kids. This was taken at the house we used to live in at South Carolina University.

Denver's a great town with lots to do. Here are two of our three kids, Jade Li and Alex II, at a Saint Patrick's Day Parade. I was on the road playing ball.

seen as a superstar and all that it means; it's really very flattering. I don't mind going to autograph signings, going places, doing things for other people. It's part of the game and it's the way I was brought up. But I feel people should respect me when I'm with my family. That's really the only thing I ask for from the fans. When I'm with my family, and I get very little time to be with them during the season, I ask that they respect me and give me the privacy and time to enjoy being with them. Sometimes you get people from somewhere else in the state who have never seen a Denver Nugget up close so you try to make exceptions, and I always do make exceptions. I try to be courteous to people. But it doesn't always work out.

I once got a letter that was sent to *The Denver Post* by a woman whose son had seen me at a park on Easter Sunday and asked me to autograph his basketball, and I refused. Well, I remember the incident very well and it wasn't quite that way. I had my little kids with me. We were playing on the swings and the park was crowded with people. He asked me to sign his ball

Jade Li and Alex II are growing up right before my eyes.

I try to spend as much time as I can with my children, like taking them to Disneyland. That's not *me in the middle.*

I can't believe how fast Alex II is growing—here he is celebrating his fourth birthday. Oh, Alex is the one on the right.

and I said, "Well, I don't want to start anything right now, but when I finish playing with my kids and I'm ready to leave the park, I see where you're playing, and I'll come over to you and sign your ball. But right now, if I sign your ball I'll have to deal with everyone who wants an autograph in the park and I want to enjoy some time with my kids." Well, the woman was very upset and wrote a letter to the newspaper. I was upset to get the letter because I tried to cooperate and still have some time with my kids. There are times when I go out of my way to sign autographs for people when I really don't have to. There are athletes who say, "No way. I'm not signing any autographs." But I make it my business after every game, if there are kids waiting, to sign each and every autograph before I leave. I don't mind doing that, even though when we're playing at home my wife and kids usually are waiting for me so we can go to dinner or something. But I feel that when I'm working, it's part of my job. But on Easter Sunday, when I'm in the park playing with my kids and having a good time, that's their time. During the season I don't see them that much to begin with. It's tough, but it comes with the job. I have to deal with it. The good part is the season lasts only seven months and then I'm off and I've got all that time to spend with them.

5
The Winning Seasons

My first couple of years with the Nuggets were somewhat lean, but after six seasons we have failed to make the playoffs only twice, in 1980–81 and 1981–82. We have made it four times and each year we seemed to go a little farther, except for the 1985–86 season when the Rockets knocked us out before we got to the semi-finals. Without a doubt, the 1984–85 season was our best—it was the best season the Nuggets have had since they've been in the NBA, and it was very satisfying. This last year had some great moments, too, but we never seemed to get over the hump. We had a lot of injuries, guys were worried about their jobs, sportswriters made guys worry about their jobs. I thought we'd go farther, but we never seemed to put it all together for a sustained period of time. But in 1984–85, everything seemed to be working for us. We won 52 regular-season games and the division championship, and then we defeated San Antonio and Utah in the playoffs before falling to the eventual champions, the Los Angeles Lakers—a grueling five-game series that, with a few breaks, we might have won.

We believed from the very beginning that year we could win. Even though we lost one of the best offensive players in the game, Kiki Vandeweghe, who I had great fun playing with and really grew to admire as a player, we got three great players in the trade that sent Kiki to Portland. We suddenly had Wayne Cooper, a big center who could block shots. We had Fat Lever, a great guard, and Calvin Natt, a forward who could score and rebound and muscle people around. You couldn't argue with the results of that trade. The facts spoke for themselves. We began with a strong pre-season, losing only a few games and developing a great winning attitude, a belief that we would win and could beat anybody. I know people say that a lot and it may sound like a cliché, but it's really the key to everything. It

---

"Alex English always looks like every shot he takes is a good shot."—**Hubie Brown, coach of the New York Knicks**

---

certainly was the key to everything we accomplished that year. You have to believe in yourself, in everything you do, and if you do, you can accomplish a great deal. I really believe that. The team felt that way all year long. We never gave up.

We had a bad year the season before, winning only 38 games and getting eliminated in the first round of the playoffs against Utah, losing the finale at home. We were determined not to let that happen again. We were not going to be a subpar team. We were no longer losing the close games at the end because we couldn't stop the other team. We were so tough defensively all of a sudden, we were giving teams the blues. I think everyone on the team sensed we were a lot tougher on defense with Calvin and Fat and Coop in there. Having Calvin there as a physical force helped us tremendously. Coop was blocking shots. T.R. and Fat were harassing the guards and driving them crazy. We were very, very good. Then we had guys like Dan Issel and Elston Turner and Bill Hanzlik coming off the bench—all those guys work hard and help inspire the rest of the team. We were the same way this year but we had an adjustment to make, losing Dan, and we had so many injuries. In 1985 we were a lot tougher with Dan coming off the bench than we had been with him starting. He did so much for us coming off the bench, giving us that instant scoring lift and getting the other teams' centers in foul trouble. We suddenly had a rebounding, shot-blocking center in Coop, and Dan will be the first to tell

It's disappointing in a "Broncos" town that we don't get bigger crowds for our games, especially earlier in the season. But the fans who do come are knowledgeable and support us with a lot of enthusiasm.

you he was primarily a scorer. He loved to shoot and he was great at drawing fouls from the big men.

Dan was really a lot of fun to play with. He had a great sense of humor and helped keep the team real loose. He was just a good old fellow who liked to have a good time. He was older than most of the players when I was there, so he didn't mix with them that much off the court. I think Kim Hughes was his best friend and the only player he hung around with. Dan basically came to work and went home when the day was over. But he liked to clown around a lot. One time Dan took out his false teeth after a practice and put them into a glass someone was drinking water from. I think it was Chopper, the trainer, and it cracked us all up. But for what Dan did on the court, I think he was one of the best ever. For his size, he was fantastic. I watched him fake Kareem out of his shoes with the same move every time, that simple head fake. Every center in the league would fall for it every time Dan used it. And he used it whenever he had a chance. Head fake, drive to the basket, or head fake, drive, pull up, shoot the jumper. He had the same moves and he produced with them every time. There was nothing complicated about Dan's style of play—it just worked. He worked hard at it, too, even though the move looked easy. It took hard work to make it go as smoothly as it did. It think we all have that kind of mechanical move to use when all else fails. But Dan was a master at it.

I am flattered by the fact that I am considered a clutch player.

Playing with Kiki was fun, too. It was fun but a lot of hard work. Neither one of us is a great rebounder and it was unfortunate we had a small center in Dan who wasn't a great rebounder, either. But Kiki is one of the best offensive players in the game. He can do a lot of things on offense and I really admire the way he plays that side of the game. He's really tough to guard—I played with him and I got to know his game. I knew when he liked to pass, when he would shoot, where he was going with his cuts or where he would take the ball. He was always moving out there. He had this great move under the basket where he nonchalantly would go away from the hoop like he wasn't even in the play and then he'd suddenly cut right back. I always tried to get the ball to him right away in that situation because I knew it was two points and maybe a foul shot. I was sorry to see him go because he was a great player, but we got three great players and a draft pick for him. That's a lot for one player, and we became a much better team as a result.

There's Dan with his feet planted firmly on the ground as usual. For a man his size, he had an amazing career with those simple, almost mechanical moves. It took us quite a while to adjust to his not being there.

I guess I'm the player the team goes to in the crunch, when the game is on the line and we need to score. The team forces that role on me and I accept it. I am considered the player who can score when we need it—although I like to consider myself a complete player who can do a lot of things out there—and I've grown accustomed to the role. It's just a state of mind, really. You have to be confident and positive about the shots when you're put in that position, but you also have to say to yourself that it's not the end of the world if you miss a shot. The world isn't going to come down on you if you miss. I am flattered by the fact that I am considered a clutch player. A lot of players run away at clutch time or disappear from the action. I welcome it. I want the ball. I get hungry for it because that's what's expected of me. It's my job. We have other players who can do it when it's needed. But I feel that is what I am paid to do. One of the biggest insults I ever got was last year after we lost to Portland in the playoffs at home when a radio commentator said I disappeared when the game was on the line. He didn't read the game correctly. It wasn't that I disappeared. It was that my team couldn't get me the ball. They were trying to get it to me but sometimes there are situations in a game when that's impossible.

THE MOST EXCRUCIATING PAIN I EVER FELT

Anyway, I'll never forget that Lakers playoff series, particularly the next-to-last game when I broke my thumb on Kareem's elbow.

It was a great game, sweet and bitter. I don't know how much farther we could have gone if I hadn't broken my thumb. If we had won that game, which we almost did anyway, even with me going out with a lot of time left in the fourth quarter, we may have won the series. We already had beaten them in L.A. in game two. I think we proved to anyone who doubted our toughness that we were for real. I think we would have been in a real strong position to beat them. The Lakers are a very good team. They won the championship that year. But I feel that when they get some really strong pressure on them, they can be beaten. If we had won that game, the series would have been tied at two games each and the pressure would have been on them to go back to the Forum and win after we had already

I try to vary my shot a little each time, put a new twist in it to catch the defenders flat-footed.

Again, when you're known as a scorer, you get clobbered a lot.

beaten them there by 22 points in the playoffs. There's no telling what would have happened.

The game was very close—it may have been tied. Kareem had just rebounded the ball and was bringing his elbow down and swinging it—it was going to hit me in the face, so I instinctively put up my hand to protect myself and the next thing I knew the bone was all out of place and sticking out. The thumb was broken in the joint. At first, I thought it had just been pushed out of place and that it wasn't that big of a deal. But as I tried to take the ball in from out of bounds a second later I felt the most excruciating pain I have ever felt in my life.

It was frustrating because we almost won, and I wondered how close we would have come if I hadn't gotten hurt. After the game I went directly to the hospital and they operated right then and there. Then in the last game in L.A., we got blown out pretty bad. We never really were in it. I don't like to over-emphasize the impact of my getting injured. I'm a key part of

The Bucks are loaded with talent. Here are two of their best: Sidney Moncrief and Paul Pressey.

the team, but I feel that when we're playing well we really are like a machine, and it was just like taking out a piece of the machine and still trying to make it function. I think it would have been the same if T.R. had gone down, or Fat Lever, or anybody.

THE 1985–86 SEASON

As far as this past season was concerned, we really felt as if our winning ways would carry over; everybody had high expectations. But injuries just about killed us. The year before we were in pretty good shape most of the year. But last season we never seemed to have everybody healthy at the same time. There were times when Coop was out, Hanzlik was out, Fat was out, Elston was out. It was just one of those years, our turn to have the guys injured. Plus, we really missed Dan coming off the bench. I think during the latter part of the year Danny Schayes and Blair made up for that. But early in the year we missed Dan's scoring a lot and it was a real adjustment that took longer than we expected. We wanted very badly to repeat as Midwest Division winners and to go even farther in the playoffs, but we just couldn't overcome all the problems.

As far as the Houston Rockets were concerned, I think their minds caught up with their young bodies. They played well—the way they are supposed to play with all the talent they have. They have two franchise players with Akeem Olajuwon and Ralph Sampson. They have strong guards. Rodney McCray is a great player, a great team player. We were the defending Midwest champions, but we just couldn't match their talent. We had the heart and desire but not the talent to match them. Those guys didn't have the heart and desire in 1984–85, so we won. This last year it all kind of caught up with them. The only bad thing that happened to us was the injuries. We had the same intensity and desire we'd had the year before, and I felt we were ready a few times to make a pretty good run on Houston and take over the division lead. But whenever we started to make a run—the year before we relied on those stretches, winning 10 or 11 in a row—we just couldn't do it. We always seemed to have a key ingredient missing. Someone was always out with an injury. We never seemed to have our full lineup out on the floor.

This is a move I have worked on for years: a running kind of one-handed hook shot going to my right. It's pretty hard to defend.

Despite all the problems, I think we gave Houston a tougher time in the playoffs than the Lakers did, and I think that says something on our behalf. In fact, I think the tough series we gave Houston prepared them to beat the Lakers the way they did. It's our style that gives us the edge, I think. We play the same run-it-up-the-floor style as the Lakers, but I think we do it better. Last year, unfortunately, our running game wasn't as effective as it was the year we won the division.

I suppose there is a changing of the guard in the West. Ralph and Akeem are the new Kareems. They are the new history-making players who are changing the game. They will endure a long time because they both can do a lot of things on the floor that make it very hard to play them. The Lakers are still a great team. They've been the power in the West for a long time. But they realize they have to make more changes to continue to be the dominating team they have been in the past. We beat them three out of five times this past year without any of our seven-footers playing.

I went to the last Laker-Rocket playoff game at the Forum because I'm basically a fan, too, and I love to watch great basketball players. There was a lot of talent on the floor that night. You really saw one of Ralph's only weaknesses as the playoffs progressed. He's got so much talent, but he needs to be more aggressive. I don't think that Olajuwon is better than Ralph, but he certainly is more aggressive. However, I have to say that some of the criticism Ralph gets really is unfair. It comes from people who don't understand the dynamics of the Rockets' game. Ralph really sacrifices a lot of his game when he and Akeem are both playing. Akeem is a great center, but if Ralph played center for the Rockets, without Akeem in there, he'd be very dominating. When Akeem sits out, Ralph usually rises to the occasion and does the job centers are supposed to do. He's a good forward, but he's much more effective playing around the basket, like Akeem. I think Ralph would be just as effective or even more so if he played center. I don't think a lot of the people who criticize Ralph really understand the situation he's in. A lot of teams would like to have Houston's problem. But Ralph is willing to sacrifice his game so the team can win, and that says a lot about him.

The whole Midwest Division is getting a lot tougher, and there is going to be pressure on us to continue to improve. We

I'll take an easy one any time I can get it.

PREPARING FOR A GAME

I've been playing so long, I guess I have a pretty consistent ritual I go through when I'm trying to get ready for a game.

On the day of a home game, I go down in the late morning for the shoot-a-round. I don't eat breakfast, and when I have lunch I usually have something light, like seafood, because it won't weigh me down. I feel light after that and I usually go home and take a nap. After I get up, I take a shower to get going and then iron some of the clothes I'll wear to the game, jeans and shirt usually. I go to the game late, because that's part of the ritual. I'll have a cup of coffee, eat some bee pollen, get taped. And all the while you're mingling and carrying on with the other guys.

We have a chapel service. After that, I'll go out and shoot to get loose. I come back in and get ready for the game. All this time you're thinking about the team you're playing, who you'll be guarding. But you have to be careful not to dwell on it too much because you don't want to get over-nervous and get too excited and get into foul trouble or something. That can easily happen. Then sometimes you can be too low key and not ever really get into the pace of the game. I've had both happen to me.

Some nights I go out and I'm ready to play, everything seems to be clicking. Other nights, no matter what you seem to do, you can't get into it. It seems impossible. The concentration just doesn't seem to be there. The shot will be off. Your hands feel like stone. Your passing is sloppy. Nothing goes right. I try not to get too excited about who the competition is. I do get up a little more for the best teams, but I try real hard to stay at the same level. You never know. I'm convinced it's just the rhythm of your body the day of the game, the time you go out to play, that dictates how you're going to do. Sometimes you can psyche yourself up and still not be able to get into it like you want to. Maybe it's the moon or biorhythms. I surely don't know.

need a big, powerful rebounder, a shot blocker, and maybe another scorer. As I said earlier, I think that Blair was coming on strong toward the end of last season, so we could be in good shape. We could start two seven-footers, like Houston does, in Cooper and Rasmussen, with Schayes being the backup. They're not as talented as Houston's big men, but nobody is, really. However, we could be competitive. The changes, I believe, are a necessity if we are to stay competitive, because the winners have that edge. Look at Boston, Houston, Los Angeles—they all have the powerful big men. Even teams like Dallas in our division are getting there. They've got lots of big guys and scorers. We don't have that. After our three big centers, I'm the next biggest man, and that's not enough to win.

THE BEST AND THE BRIGHTEST

This seems like a good time to offer some comments on other players, past and present, whom I have enjoyed watching and playing against and respect. There are lots of them, but a few stand out in my mind.

I guess my all-time favorite was Bobby Dandridge, the great Bucks forward I mentioned earlier. Besides helping me adjust to life in the pros, he played one the sweetest and best games I ever saw. He was small and very underrated, but I think he was one of the greatest forwards ever to play the game. Whenever someone like Julius Erving came to town, Bobby used to kill those guys. He loved to play against the best. People today don't know who he is, since he has been out of the game for several years. You say Elgin Baylor and everybody knows the name. But Bobby Dandridge was one of the best. He had this sweet shot, pulling the ball back behind his head, making it impossible to block. When I started on the Bucks he was one of the oldest players on the team and I became kind of his understudy. He had played on the Bucks' championship team with Kareem in 1970–71, and I learned an awful lot just watching him play. He was very confident. He knew what he could do. His shot was almost always off balance, so it was hard to know when it was coming. It looked like he'd be walking, taking steps, because he would shoot it when you didn't expect it. He was deceptive and different. We have some similarities in that regard. I'm also a small forward who believes in himself, and a lot of that I got just from watching him play and listening to him talk. A lot of his inner confidence rubbed off on me. He wasn't a boastful

*Scoring is what my teammates
expect me to do.*

1986 WESTERN CONFERENCE ALL-STARS

Front Row (left to right): Kareem Abdul-Jabbar, James Worthy, Coach Pat Riley, Earvin Johnson, Alvin Robertson, Ralph Sampson.

Back row (left to right): Trainer Doug Atkinson, Assistant Coach Randy Pfund, Akeem Olajuwon, Adrian Dantley, Clyde Drexler, Rolando Blackman, Artis Gilmore, Alex English, Marques Johnson, Assistant Coach Bill Bertka.

You have to feel proud to play in an All-Star game with great players like these guys.

guy; he was kind of quiet. You just picked up strength from him because he had a great sense of what he could do on the basketball court.

Another small forward I admired and loved to watch was Jamaal Wilkes, when he played with the Lakers. He was another one I'd put at the top of the list of the toughest and most underrated. I admired him because of his quiet but strong style and for the way he carried himself on and off the floor. He was a leader by the example he set. He was very tough to play against. Kareem is fantastic, of course, the best center ever to

Alex II thought he was cool behind-the-scenes at the NBA All-Star game, but he's still not as cool as his dad—yet.

Part of being an NBA All-Star is doing some publicity work.

play the game. You have to admire Kareem for all the years he has put in and for all the great play. But when we played the Lakers, at least after Jamaal Wilkes had gone, it was the whole team I got up for rather than any one individual. Another tough one to play against was John Johnson of the Seattle Supersonics. He was very strong and physical.

There are great new players coming into the game all the time. Besides Ralph Sampson and Akeem and the others I've mentioned, I think Rolando Blackman of the Dallas Mavericks is one of the best newcomers. James Worthy is definitely one of the best forwards in the league. He has such a quick start and runs so well, he's very hard to defend against. Rodney McCray is another one. He sacrifices some of his game to play within the team structure and he doesn't get the recognition he deserves. I think Mike Woodson of Sacramento is very tough. I'd rate him with Rolando Blackman as far as big guards are concerned. Xavier McDaniel is going to be one of the best players in the NBA one day soon. If he can control himself and get it together, he'll be one of the very best there is. He has a lot of heart and great desire and he's very, very strong. Alvin Robertson, the San Antonio guard, is another great young player. There are a lot of great guards in our division who are overshadowed by Magic Johnson, as far as getting publicity— Fat Lever, Johnny Moore, and when he's healthy, Lewis Lloyd. If I had to choose just one player to build a franchise around, I think I'd pick Akeem or Ralph. Akeem is probably the most dominating center in the game today, and that includes Kareem, because Olajuwon can do more things on the floor at this point in his career than Kareem can anymore. Patrick Ewing would be the third player I might choose to build a franchise around. He'll be a great one and may surpass them all before he's finished. Michael Jordan is unbelievable. It's amazing the things he can do on the floor. Chicago has a lot of talent, in fact, and may be a powerhouse if they can add a little to complement Michael. They need a center who can do the job defensively. It's too bad Quentin Dailey went down with his drug problem because I think he was one of the most talented of the big shooting guards in the league.

Which I suppose brings me to a delicate subject: drugs in the NBA. Unfortunately, it's something we can't avoid talking about.

You have to look the ball into the basket, even on the so-called easy ones.

6
Sure, Pro Athletes Are Pampered

First we need to talk about the lifestyle of an NBA player. I love the game. It's been great to me and I enjoy playing. But it's not as easy or as glamorous as some people would believe.

It's a grind a lot of the time. You get up at all hours of the morning to catch a bus to go to the airport. You're half asleep. You check in at the airport. You don't have enough time to pay your bills, so someone has to do that for you. You're always running, it seems, to catch a bus or an airplane. You eat breakfast on the fly. You wait on the plane and hope you can fall asleep. It's like you don't really know where you are. Sometimes after a game, the adrenalin is flowing so much you can't fall asleep. I've stayed up until two or three in the morning, tossing and turning because I couldn't sleep. If it was a really big game, you're so excited it seems that it's impossible to fall asleep. If you finally fall asleep, it seems that as soon as you do the phone rings and someone is waking you up to get on another bus or another plane. I usually sleep on the plane because by that time I'm dead. Then you get to the next city you have to play in and you try to sleep most of the day so you can be rested for the game that night. So you get up late in the afternoon and feel all drowsy and disoriented. Your legs may be

111

sore from the game the night before. But almost as soon as you get up you have to start getting yourself mentally prepared for the game that night. And all the time you're missing your family because you don't get to see them much when you're on the road.

But, yes, I guess we are pampered somewhat. We're pampered because we almost have to be. We have someone taking care of our travel arrangements and our bags—we don't have the time with the type of schedule we're on. We stay at the best hotels and eat at the finest restaurants. It's all part of the deal. After all, that's how most professional entertainers live and

"Alex is such a prolific offensive player and plays in such a running style that you have to cut down his opportunities. He's averaged over 32 points a game against us, so he's a major concern. But one player can't stop another all by himself in this league. It needs to be more of a team defense, we have to get somebody to run at him. That's difficult with Alex, because 60 percent of his shots are running one-handers."—**Kenny Carr, forward of the Portland Trailblazers**

that's what we are—entertainers. But it's up to the individual to keep it in the right perspective and not get carried away with it all. This only lasts a short time—it's fleeting and soon it will be over.

But there are a lot of temptations for guys and, sadly, one of them is drugs. I think the drug problem had really gotten out of hand in all segments of our society by the early 1980s—lawyers, doctors, everybody. But I'm glad the issue has been put up front the way it has so people could see it and really be made aware of it. I think that spotlight actually saved a lot of guys' lives and marriages and families. It's better that it's up front like that and not in the closet where it never gets discussed. It's something I feel we all need to be concerned about, not just basketball players or other professional athletes. I was watching the evening news not long ago and two net-

During the 1984–85 playoffs against the Lakers, I broke my thumb on Kareem's elbow.

works had stories about this new form of cocaine called crack. I had never even heard of it until a week earlier.

Drugs: we all need to be concerned and I am very concerned about the effect they have had on my profession. For one thing, a lot of people are saying, "Hey, I'm not going to go see a bunch of drug addicts play basketball. I'm not going to support their habit." Well, that's not the kind of publicity we need. But what those critics fail to see is that it isn't as bad or as widespread as the press reported. It's not 100 percent of the players in the league, it isn't even up to 75 percent. It could be 20 to 25 percent. I can honestly say there is not one guy on the Nuggets who uses drugs or anyone I would even suspect of using drugs. And I think a lot of that has to do with the educational programs and other things the league and players' association have done to try to deal with this problem. Basketball was the first professional sport to have a drug program as part of the agreement with the players, and I think that says a lot about our role in professional sports as the pioneers in dealing with this problem.

It's OK if your defender knows, or thinks he knows, you're going to make the same move a lot, as I do to the right. He still has to stop you, even if he expects it.

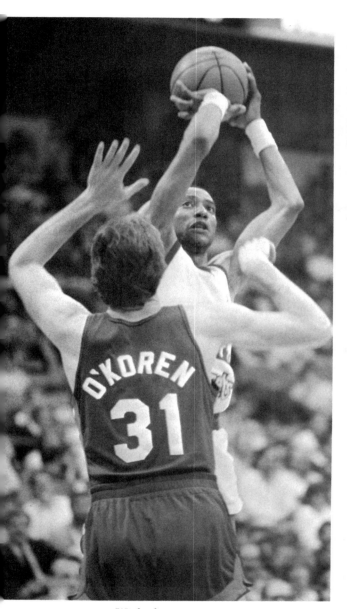

With the many commitments and the pressure of being under the lights, the life of an NBA player is not as glamorous as it seems.

As far as banning guys from the league for life after their third offense with drugs, well, they're really kicked out for only two years, not for life. But I suppose for all intents and purposes you may as well say it is for life, because I don't think a guy can come back after two years off—the game is too tough and it's such a competitive market. There are so many good players coming out of college to take their place. Anyway, at one time I thought that punishment was a bit harsh, that it was unfair. But I think if a guy really cares, he should listen to the warnings and work hard to pull himself together. Drug addiction, you know, is a disease, and it should be treated as a

---

Drugs: we all need to be concerned and I am very worried about the effect they have had on my profession.

---

disease. When you confront a person and tell him his life is in jeopardy, that his livelihood and his family and his marriage are at stake, he should be concerned enough to work on it. If you make a person aware of the outcome if he continues to use drugs . . . . I mean, everybody should know what he can lose. It's really quite clear—it should change him. It's a disease, but the question becomes, How many chances do you give a person to help himself? If I were a drug addict and I knew my life and my career and even my means of getting the drug were jeopardized, my family and everything else would make me stop and think and give it up. Some people are made of different stuff, though, and I guess there needs to be someone telling them, "Hey, that's it. It's over for you."

I don't want to sound insensitive, but I do have a hard time understanding why people can't fight drug addiction a little more successfully. They read and hear and see so much about how devastating it can be and how they have so much to lose. I do think one thing that's definitely needed is a better after-care program. You can't take a guy and put him through a 30-day program and just pop him out on the street and expect everything to be okay after that. I think what happened to Michael Ray Richardson, the talented guard from Denver who played for the New Jersey Nets, is a good example of that and is a real tragedy. People who have this problem need constant monitoring and help.

I'm glad the issue of drugs in sports has been brought out in the open.

We are entertainers on the court, always trying to please the crowd.

I can honestly say there is not one guy on the Nuggets who uses drugs or anyone I would even suspect of using drugs.

I've heard people ask what effect all of this has on the little kids and young people who tend to idolize their favorite pro athletes and place them on a pedestal, especially since they see that some of these guys who do use drugs come back and perform at what seems to be the top of their game. But we don't always see the hidden effects of drug use. Walter Davis, the great player on the Phoenix Suns, scored 42 points one night and put himself into a treatment center the next day. There's an inconsistency in the performance of a guy on drugs that the kid may not see. Paranoia, the erratic behavior, the detachment from people. How does this guy act when he's not on the court? How does he deal with his wife and family? How does he deal with everyday stress and pressures? I've been around guys who were heavy drug users and it always seems to catch up with them.

A poem given to Dick Martin, a columnist, the day before I was traded from the Indiana Pacers to the Denver Nuggets:

From hotel to hotel,
Forgetting the city you're in,
Seeing faces
That resemble other faces,
Traveling all the time,
Not at the speed of light
But only a few mph less.
Losing your key,
Paying incidentals,
Playing at home tonight,
New York tomorrow
And Philly the next day
And coming home
To play the day after that.
Spraining an ankle,
Teamwork, footwork,
No work.
Talking to reporters,
NBA and CBS.
Expanding your knowledge.
Frustration.
Summer vacation,
Some relaxation.
Training camps that are boring,
Jock straps, sneakers,
And two wrist bands.
Coaches coaching.
Players playing.
Phony people, good people,
And people.

Denver is a community that genuinely seems to appreciate your involvement with charities and other civic functions, and that's important to me.

But I do think sports is coming to grips with the problem a little faster than the rest of society and can actually serve as a model. I think athletes have to because we have such a high profile. If people can read and see stories of athletes fighting back, of being the kinds of heroes that kids expect us to be—I think it will be a painful but good thing in the long run.

There's no doubt about it—drugs have been the biggest problem that has shaken the sports world to date. I read an article not long ago that speculated that the reason the Edmonton Oilers didn't win the Stanley Cup again was that the team had a drug problem. They said the same thing about the New England Patriots after they lost last year's Super Bowl to the Chicago Bears. People make a big deal about it when athletes

are implicated because we're so much in the public eye. So we have to make a special effort to deal with it if we are to maintain the integrity of the sports we're involved in.

Then again, society tends to be pretty unrealistic about what it expects of athletes. I think sometimes people don't really see us as human. They feel we can't be regular persons with regular weaknesses, that we can't possibly have a drug or alcohol problem, that we can't go through a divorce, that we can't have the same foibles and problems that everyday people have because they put us on a pedestal. But that's unrealistic. We are everyday people. We breathe the same air, we eat the same foods. We may make a lot more money than most people, but underneath it all we are regular people. A lot of us have very similar and simple backgrounds. We come from poor families. Most of the black players come from the ghetto.

There's no doubt that athletes are pampered a little bit. We need to better realize the tremendous opportunity and responsibility we have in being able to make very good livings playing games we love. But the public also needs to realize that we really aren't that different from everybody else.

Players must be aware that they are idols not only on the court, but off the court as well.

7
Odds and Ends

Well, even though I talked about wanting to be an astronaut, I know that's not going to happen. I think a lot about what I want to do when my playing days are over. I haven't really yet decided, although I know one thing is certain: I'd like to take it easy for a while. Basketball is a punishing game and I'd like to relax. It would be the first time in a long time, since I will have played college or pro ball nearly 15 years after this season.

I've prepared myself, so I know I won't have to go out and work for a living when I quit, but I know I'll want to find something to keep me busy. I don't want to sit around and do nothing. At one point, when I was in college, I thought I'd go into politics someday, but that's definitely out. Politics has too much politics in it. I just don't think I could kiss someone's —— just to get some campaign contributions or support for one of my positions. Plus, campaigning is a grind. I don't want to be on the road after I finish playing. I want to stay home and enjoy my family. I'm sure I'll do a lot of things that basketball has kept me from doing, like enjoying Christmas in Columbia with my family, things like that. But I've loved the game and I'm sure I'll miss playing when it's over.

"When I visualize Alex English, I see a mass of elbows and knees knotted up like a rubber band. Suddenly it contracts, and out flies a basketball, floating like a butterfly toward the net. Seemingly it doesn't make a sound as it drops through the basket." —Buddy Martin, *The Denver Post*, sports columnist

Vanessa and I recently toured China with friends and some other NBA players.

While in China, we took a tour of the nuclear underground shelters.

Maurice Lucas, a fellow-NBA player, loves to joke around even while posing on the Great Wall.

The Denver fans really support and appreciate me and that means a lot. I also get a chance to do things in the community and I enjoy that.

It's kind of like someone who is drunk and gets stopped by a police officer and is told to walk a straight line. If you veer off that line, you're going to be in trouble. That's how basketball has been. Or just living in general. You struggle to stay on that straight line and not diverge, try to live the way you are supposed to.

I know, also, that I'll keep writing poetry, and here's a poem to leave you with. It's called "Wishin," and it's from *Sometimey Feelins Sometime*, which was published in 1979.

Staring at the sky
Always wondering why
God didn't make it
So that I could fly
High in the sky.
I would fly
Going places that
I shouldn't be,
But only because I'd
Want to see.
Maybe God should
Have made me a tree
Then I could live
An eternity
Then I know a lot
I would see
But he made me
a Man, and I'll
Let it be
Cause I can still
See
Even if short it
Be

1,000-Point Club

1,972, Alex English, Forward, 6'8", 190 lbs., Columbia, S.C.

Season	G	Field Goals	
1972–73	29	189-368	.514
1973–74	27	209-395	.529
1974–75	28	199-359	.554
1975–76	27	258-468	.551
Totals	**111**	**855-1590**	**.538**

1985-86 Season Totals

G	FG-FGA	PCT	FT-FTA	PCT	O-T
81	951-1888	.504	511-593	.862	192-405

Free Throws		Pts.	Avg.
44-70	.629	442	14.6
75-112	.670	493	18.3
49-77	.636	447	16.0
94-134	.701	610	22.6
262-393	**.667**	**1972**	**17.8**

AST	PTS	AVG	3-Pnt. FG-FGA	PCT	PF	STL	TO	BLK
320	2414	29.8	1-5	.200	235	73	249	29

1986 Post-Season Totals

Nuggets-Rockets/Six-Game Series Statistics

FG	FGA	Pct.	FT	FTA	Pct.	Reb. Avg.
68	140	.486	39	44	.886	4.0

Nuggets/1986 Playoff Statistics

FG	FGA	Pct.	FT	FTA	Pct.	Reb. Avg.
106	129	.463	61	71	.859	3.5

Ast. Avg.	PF-D	Stl.	TO	BS	Avg.	Hi
4.0	16-0	1	12	4	29..2	42

Ast. Avg.	PF-D	Stl.	TO	BS	Avg.	Hi
5.2	29-0	4	28	4	27.3	432

Career Totals

Regular Season

Year/Team	GP	MIN	FGM-FGA	PCT.	FTM-FTA	PCT.
76–77/Milw.	60	648	132–277	.477	46–60	.767
77–78/Milw.	82	1552	343–633	.542	104–143	.727
78–79/Indiana	81	2696	563–1113	.511	173–230	.752
79–80/Ind.–Den.	78	2401	553–1113	.497	210–266	.789
80–81/Denver	81	3093	768–1555	.494	390–459	.850
81–82/Denver	82	3015	855–1553	.551	372–443	.840
82–83/Denver	82	2988	959–1857	.516	406–490	.829
83–84/Denver	82	2870	907–1714	.529	352–427	.824
84–85/Denver	81	2924	939–1812	.518	383–462	.829

Playoffs

Year/Team	GP	MIN	FGM-FGA	PCT.	FTM-FTA	PCT.
77–78/Milw.	9	208	48–78	.615	25–32	.781
81–82/Denver	3	118	26–55	.473	6–7	.857
82–83/Denver	7	270	67–150	.447	47–53	.887
83–84/Denver	5	203	60–102	.588	25–28	.893
84–85/Denver	14	536	163–304	.536	97–109	.890

OFF-DEF	REB	AST	PF-D	STL	BS	PTS.	AVG.
68-100	168	25	78-0	17	18	310	5.2
144-251	395	129	178-1	41	55	790	9.6
253-402	655	271	214-3	70	78	1299	16.0
269-336	605	224	206-0	73	62	1318	16.9
273-373	646	290	255-2	106	98	1929	23.8
207-348	555	433	261-2	87	120	2082	25.4
263-338	601	397	235-1	116	126	2326	28.4
216-248	464	406	252-3	83	95	2167	26.4
203-255	458	344	259-1	101	46	2262	27.9
16-23	42	13	20-0	6	7	121	13.4
8-15	23	17	6-0	3	3	58	19.3
20-24	44	42	21-0	4	7	181	25.9
16-24	40	28	17-0	3	2	145	29.0
36-56	92	63	40-1	17	4	423	30.2